CW01614116

STRES

KEVIN GOURNAY

ASSET BOOKS

ASSET BOOKS LTD., DORKING, SURREY RH4 2TU, UNITED KINGDOM

STRESS MANAGEMENT:

A GUIDE TO COPING WITH STRESS

KEVIN GOURNAY

ASSET BOOKS

1 Paper Mews, 330 High Street
Dorking , Surrey RH4 2TU

A catalogue record for this book is available from the British Library.

ISBN 1 900179 00 8

Printed and bound in Great Britain by Prisma Press

CONTENTS

INTRODUCTION - What is Stress?

Stress is a word which is widely used, but poorly defined. Everyone would admit to having occasions when they are 'under stress' or 'stressed out' or just plain 'stressed'. As a word it is probably only in the last couple of decades that it has come into such universal usage, but the feelings associated with this condition are probably as old as the human race itself. Textbooks give a range of definitions of what stress is and various researchers have looked at it in different ways. Perhaps the best way of considering the word is to see it from slightly different perspectives.

Firstly, stress can be seen as those factors around us (also known as stressors), which are the cause of an unpleasant reaction. Stressors may, for example, be a job, a person or a polluted atmosphere. Stress can also be more general than that. It can be a set of events or circumstances.

Secondly, stress can be seen as the individual's way of reacting or responding to stresses or stressors. This stress response in turn comprises four separate components, (i.e. physical, thinking, behaviour and mood). We will return to these responses in more detail.

The third way of seeing stress is to view it as a total process involving both the external stressors and our individual responses to them. What is interesting here is that there is tremendous variation in the way that different individuals respond to the same set of external stressors. This observation thus highlights the difference between people who cope with stress and people who don't cope with stress. Again, this will be referred to later.

INDIVIDUAL RESPONSES TO EXTERNAL STRESSORS

Individual responses to stress can take different forms and can be considered in terms of their effects on the physical state, behavioural patterns or on thinking processes or mood (Table 1).

1. Physical responses

Our physical responses to stress are underpinned by the body's production of adrenaline. Very simply, stress produces a 'fight-or-flight' response and, as part of this, the body produces the hormone adrenaline. The release of adrenaline leads to a number of changes in the body which are basically healthy and adaptive. More fundamentally this response is our central survival mechanism and puts the body into a state of optimum preparedness and, certainly, if there is real danger and either fight or flight is necessary, these changes (which are also known generally as an increase in arousal) will lead the body to perform to its best.

However, if the stresses producing this reaction do not lead to any physical response (i.e. if physical fight or flight does not occur), the body will remain in this 'ready' or 'wound up' state for some time. This may occur, for example, if a work colleague makes you very angry and you are unable to vent your anger in some way. Another case may be a situation in which you are working to a deadline, but you are constantly interrupted by a ringing telephone. Thus, although you are trying hard, you are unable to act as you wish. If such instances are repeated, the reactions build and the physical manifestations remain.

The classic physical responses to stress are an increase in heart rate and blood pressure, an increase in the depth of breathing, tension of the muscles, dilation of the pupil of the eye and an increase in the activity of the gastrointestinal tract. In the longer term, these physical changes can cause a number of medical conditions, some of which can be fatal. For example, an increase in blood pressure sustained over a period of time, can lead to heart attack or stroke; the increased activity of the gastrointestinal tract can lead to stomach ulcers; muscle tension can cause all kinds of aches and pains and over-breathing can lead to a number of distressing symptoms, some of which will be discussed in greater detail later in this book (page 27). Furthermore, the physical manifestations of stress have been linked with a number of other diseases such as asthma, skin conditions, and even cancer.

The state of physical tension caused by the physical responses to stress can, in many people, lead to excessive drinking or smoking. Simply these habits produce, in the short term at least, a reduction in physical stress. However, in the long term, both of these habits can have disastrous consequences on health.

The physical manifestations of stress have, in the past, been treated using tranquillisers, and in recent times, the benzodiazepines (e.g. Valium, Librium, Ativan, Mogadon) were prescribed in very large numbers for treatment of the physical symptoms. By the middle of the 1980's, it was estimated that there were 26,000,000 prescriptions per year for this class of tranquilliser and it was estimated that one in ten British males received a regular prescription for a benzodiazepine.

Among women the rates were even higher. Overall, one in five adult women received at least one prescription for a benzodiazepine tranquilliser in any one year and in women over the age of 40, this

TABLE 1 Examples of individual responses to external stressors

Physical responses	Increased heart rate and blood pressure Increased breathing - rate and depth Muscle tension Dilation of the pupils Increased gastrointestinal activity Excessive drinking and smoking Appetite change - may be gain or loss
Thinking responses	**Initially:** Thinking speed increases **Longer term:** Difficulty in attending to information Reduced ability to concentrate Problems with information processing Increasing forgetfulness Reduced recall of important information Negative thinking Poor self-perception
Behavioural responses	Avoiding stressful situations Withdrawal from social activities Loss of sense of enjoyment Changed sexual behaviour - usually loss of desire Irritability and aggressive behaviour Excessive drinking and smoking Over- or under-eating May lead to drug taking Disrupted sleep Proneness to accidents
Mood responses	Mood changes - misery, pessimism, dejection and feeling that life is not worth living Depression Irritability At its extreme, suicidal feelings/actions.

figure was one in three. The consequences of large scale benzodiazepine addiction are now becoming clear and certainly it is now known that literally millions of people have led very impoverished lives because of the long-term consumption of, and addiction to, tranquillisers.

2. Thinking Responses

An excess of stress induces changes in one's thinking. In the short term this may be adaptive, so that an increase in the speed of thought will assist one in a situation where an immediate response is needed. However, in the long term, stress causes a number of different thinking problems.

To begin with there is often a difficulty in attending to information and great difficulty in concentrating. In turn, this leads to problems with all information processing and there is increasing forgetfulness and difficulty recalling important information. This is not a problem of memory in itself, but rather is associated with the over-activity of the thinking process and the difficulties in concentration.

Over a long period of time one of the most pronounced characteristics of thinking in stressed individuals is that it will become negative and catastrophic. The continuing catastrophising is, of course, the main element of worry and this, in turn, may have a profound effect on sleep. In addition to catastrophising, this pattern of negative thinking will lead to poor perception of oneself and one's own abilities. Thus, eventually one could find oneself in the throes of a downward spiral which eventually perpetuates itself.

3. Behavioural responses

There are a range of ways in which we react behaviourally to stress.

In the first instance we may simply choose to avoid those situations which we know cause us stress. However avoidance may not be helpful as a long-term strategy as this can lead to a pattern. The more we try to avoid such situations the more anticipation may build.

For example, ask yourself what happens when you put off making a 'phone call to someone from whom you are expecting a difficult response. The longer you put it off, the more difficult it becomes. We then begin to anticipate the situation when it looms up again. Further avoidance leads to more anticipation and a consequent increase in physical apprehension which may cause muscle tension, headache or palpitations.

Behavioural avoidance may also manifest itself in withdrawal from social activities, so that we begin to deprive ourselves of the very things which help keep us happy and engaged and which add to the quality of our lives. In turn, we lose our sense of enjoyment and life may seem very flat. Severe avoidance behaviour may produce a clinical phobia which can, at times, become permanent.

Other behavioural changes which result from exposure to stress may include difficulties in sleep, changes in our activity levels and an over-proneness to accidents. People who are under stress may sometimes change their food intake. Over-eating is often used as a way of relaxing. Conversely, stressful periods in life may lead to appetite loss and an inability to eat because of the nausea which may accompany the physical over-activity of arousal. Thus stress can lead to either weight gain or weight loss.

Stress may lead to changes in interest in sexual activity and usually there is a decrease in desire. However, occasionally, sexual desire is increased although in this case, sexual performance is often impaired.

Because of the increase in physical arousal, other common behavioural manifestations of stress include increases in irritability and aggressive behaviour; these may be the only sign to others that anything is amiss. This aggression can be shown to colleagues at work in the form of curt verbal responses, but it can also reach dangerous levels. For example, drivers who are under stress may use their cars aggressively or may become involved in altercations with others. This constitutes what is now known as 'Driver Rage' or 'Road Rage'. Driving itself may be stressful, with exposure to traffic jams and others driving badly being obvious triggers. However, more often than not, the driver who behaves in a stressed way was probably in a high level of arousal before he or she stepped into the car!

Of course, all of the behavioural manifestations of stress can be linked to patterns of other problematic behaviour such as excessive smoking, drinking and drug taking (both legal and illegal). These behaviours certainly have their own deleterious consequences and often lead to another set of vicious circles.

4. Mood responses

Eventually, after prolonged periods of stress, one's mood can be affected and severe depression may be one of the worst consequences. At its extreme, this can lead to suicidal feelings and actions but, at lower levels, there is misery, pessimism, dejection and a feeling that life is not worth living. It has recently been recognised that up to a quarter of the population experience significant periods of depression in their lives and, as such, depression is one of the major unrecognised sources of illness in our society.

Although depression often results from prolonged stress it can, of course, be an illness in its own right resulting from a mixture of social, psychological and physical factors.

Burnout

For many health professionals, teachers, and others engaged in human services, burnout is the ultimate problem associated with stress. Jobs which in themselves produce stress - for example working in emotionally charged situations, having a high level of work load, needing to meet tight deadlines and working with others who are stressed themselves - increases the chance of burnout. Burnout is a phrase which encompasses a number of symptoms but researchers categorise these into three core components (Table 2).

First there is emotional exhaustion. In this state the person feels unable to give any more emotionally of themselves to the job or to those around them. This very often leads to the blunting of relationships in one's social and personal life. This blunting may make the person believe that they have permanently lost their ability 'to feel' which, in turn, may create dejection and poor self-worth.

Secondly there is depersonalisation. This condition is often manifested by treating others in an uncaring or callous fashion. It may be typified by a nurse working in an intensive care setting who pays more attention to the machines than to the people who are connected to them. An affected person may be dismissive of those around them, and if they themselves are openly upset by some aspect of this often harrowing work, the person suffering depersonalisation may make unkind comments or even display open contempt towards

TABLE 2	Core components in burnout
	Emotionally drained, unable 'to give any more'
	Feelings of depersonalisation
	Perceptions of inadequacy

others. Another example of this may be found in a teacher who develops an obsessive preoccupation with assessment or some other bureaucratic trappings of the job, while at the same time ignoring the needs of his or her students.

The third feature of burnout is the perceived inadequacy of professional accomplishment. This may be exemplified by a teacher saying 'there's no point in trying to teach these kids anything, you can't get through to them, it's just not worth trying any more'. Sometimes perceived inadequacy may be betrayed by a harsh cynicism about standards in general or the standards of one's contemporaries, but the harshest criticism is usually reserved for oneself. The person sees no real results for their efforts, although ironically, they are often normally seen as exemplars of excellent practice!

How can burnout be prevented or treated?

First and foremost, professionals and their managers need to recognise that the problem is extremely prevalent. Research has shown that a high level of face to face contact with, for example, patients or students, can lead to greater emotional exhaustion. Therefore this phenomenon can be partly addressed by the manager who ensures that, where possible, there is a variation in the work programme. This can perhaps be achieved with some rotation of administrative responsibilities between workers.

Research has also shown that there is need to recognise that simple social support can help to prevent burnout. Staff need to be given the opportunity to discuss difficulties amongst themselves; simply helping each other may be the most important preventative strategy.

Attention to the work environment has also been shown to be a crucial factor in prevention of burnout. For example, the provision of exercise facilities and attention to decor, ventilation and lighting can all reduce the probability of burnout occurring. In addition, there is increasing awareness that long periods of exposure to computer screens may be stressful so that operators need frequent breaks in their work pattern.

Fatigue

Fatigue is one of the commonest symptoms of stress. Sometimes it is the main symptom and sufferers may repeatedly visit their doctor saying that they feel tired all the time and have no energy. The precise mechanisms underlying this are unclear, but one simple reason is that, if you are in a state of high arousal, your muscles are continually tense; the feeling of fatigue stems from this tension.

An increased susceptibility to minor infections, such as colds and other viruses, is often associated with fatigue. Research has shown that stress may adversely affect the immune system, thus causing an increased susceptibility to infection; furthermore such infections may lead in themselves to post-viral fatigue. In such fatigue states, people often feel depressed and more anxious and thus perpetuating a vicious circle.

It is not uncommon to see people who suffer from chronic stress reporting a history of many years of feeling tired all the time and of having sought numerous forms of medical advice without any result.

More optimistically, there is research evidence to show that some simple strategies can improve the subjective feeling of tiredness. Surprisingly perhaps, regular exercise carried out at least three times a week can improve one's state of well-being and tiredness will recede (see page 30 for more detail). It is common knowledge that a hard day at work - where you have been subjected to lots of stress - may leave you feeling totally exhausted. However, in this case, physical activity of some kind may restore your energy. Exercise as a form of treatment has been put to the test in various research trials and while, for some people, it does not provide the answer, it does seem that the majority of people will benefit from this approach.

Another simple strategy is relaxation training (again described in further detail later). Learning to relax may undoubtedly help discharge some of the physical effects of stress from the body.

More often than not fatigue is present with other symptoms of stress and the indications are that a total approach to the problem is needed. You will find in later pages that a number of strategies are described and it will probably be necessary for you to try a combination of these to deal with the problem effectively.

Post-Traumatic Stress Disorder

As this book may be read by nurses, police officers and teachers amongst others, it is possible that some readers will suffer post-traumatic stress disorder. It is often wrongly assumed that this is only found in the victims of major disasters and catastrophes. However, many people suffer a great deal from exposure to many of the traumatic events which are now, unfortunately, so common in our society.

For example, nurses may witness tragic and sudden deaths, they may, like police officers, need to handle bodies after accidents or may simply suffer form the effects of exposure to relentless human suffering. Teaching, once a sedate profession, now carries its own risks. Many teachers have unfortunately been subjected to violent assaults by pupils or parents. Specific major incidents or, more often, a relentless accumulation of minor incidents, may lead to the development of this disorder.

The medical definition of post-traumatic stress emphasises that the person has been exposed to a traumatic event in which they experienced, witnessed or were confronted with an event or events that involved threatened death, serious injury or a threat to the physical integrity of themselves or others. The response itself involves intense fear, helplessness or horror. Recently these concepts have been widened to include the witnessing of traumatic events and there is no doubt that there are literally tens of thousands of people affected by such problems.

One of the commonest forms of post-traumatic stress disorder is that affecting those people who have been involved in road traffic accidents, even those which do not cause significant injury. In these cases the person will have often thought that they were about to die and so become very frightened.

Several groups of symptoms make up post-traumatic stress. For example, sufferers often experience recurrent and intrusive recollections of the event which may occur during dreams or even in the waking state.

There may be great distress when reconfronting circumstances similar to those in which the original trauma took place (such as driving close to the site of the original accident). In addition, the person may experience a numbing of their general responses and show a markedly diminished interest in their usual activities. Sometimes they feel detached or estranged from others and they often have a foreshortened future. A person may experience difficulty in falling asleep, or have outbursts of irritability or anger, finding it difficult to concentrate; they may be constantly aware of possible danger in the environment.

Severe or moderately severe post-traumatic stress is usually recognised, but many people who have lower levels of the problem continue to suffer because their problems are not recognised and so receive no attention. Thus, for example, a teacher who has been assaulted may return to work and stay in a continually frightened state and become chronically unhappy. The responses of colleagues are sometimes not very sympathetic and one often hears statements such as 'She should have got over it by now'. Post-traumatic stress disorder often leads to an excessive use of alcohol or other drugs usually in an attempt to numb the distress.

Post-traumatic stress disorder is a condition, which needs to be recognised and treated professionally. The reason for describing the problem here is simply that you may have a colleague who is showing signs of the condition, but who is not receiving professional help.

It may therefore be helpful, albeit difficult, if you could play a part in helping them to recognise their problem and thereby access the help they need.

WHAT IS STRESS MANAGEMENT?

Nearly every large organisation, be it the health service, multinational companies, education authorities, or the police force, now runs courses in stress management. This is, of course, an excellent sign that the problem is now being recognised as a universal phenomenon and one which is now carrying much less stigma. However, stress management programmes vary considerably in their content and thence probably in their effectiveness.

It should be emphasised at the outset that many of the best ways of managing stress can be engineered by oneself, without necessarily having to access professional help or attend an expensive course. Many of the principles of stress management are based on common sense, but there are many different approaches and most individuals need a combination rather than a single approach. Thus, it is folly to assume that if one does a relaxation exercise every day, this will cure stress or, similarly, that attending an evening class will prove to be a panacea for complex work problems.

What follows is a discussion of some of the most common methods of stress reduction. This is by no means all-inclusive; neither is each section intended to be totally comprehensive. The discussion of each of the approaches to the problem provides, firstly, a checklist of things which need to be considered and, secondly, a description of the key principles in each of the approaches.

As I will emphasise below, professional treatment is occasionally necessary and if a concerted attempt to deal with stress using a suitable combination of the approaches is not effective, one should consider seeking professional advice. However, for most people, self

TABLE 3 **Components of stress management**

- Problem solving - sharing problems
- Managing type-A behaviour
- Improved time management
- Relaxation training
- Over-breathing and dealing with hyperventilation
- Exercise
- Identifying negative thoughts
- Improving sleeping patterns
- Improving eating patterns
- Control of alcohol consumption
- Reducing smoking
- Assertion training
- Hobbies

help is very effective and there are now a number of research studies which show that simple principles can be taught via books, videos and computer programmes. Professor Isaac Marks at London's Institute of Psychiatry has researched this area for a number of years and has shown that even when treating people with severe phobias and obsessions, self-help methods can be as effective as professional help in a majority of cases. Therefore read the following carefully; make some notes; discuss what you are doing with a partner or friend and don't give up!

Problem Solving - A problem shared

Discussing one's difficulties with others is perhaps the starting point for most stress management programmes. Simply sharing your problem with someone else can be a very effective remedy for stress. Indeed, the role of social support in a range of emotional difficulties has been shown to be a crucial variable. For example, various studies have shown that a close confiding relationship may prevent the occurrence of depression. Sometimes people feel that support of this type should be labelled 'counselling'. However, to professionalise the simple process of one human being sharing their troubles with another is, for the most part, unnecessary. Counselling is an ill-defined phenomenon which, despite many claims for its effectiveness, and the presence of several organisations representing counsellors, has very little evidence attesting to an effect over and above simple social support.

However, there are now forms of counselling which have been better defined and researched. For example, a brief method, which takes 4-6 sessions and known as 'problem-oriented counselling', has been shown to be effective for dealing with stressful life events. It is, therefore, perhaps worth devoting a little space to looking at the central components of this interesting approach.

- *List your problems:* Do this initially on your own, or if you feel it helpful with your partner or a friend
- *Brainstorm solutions:* Beside each problem write all possible solutions, even those which seem to be most way out
- *Option appraisal:* Look at each of the possible solutions very carefully and then consider the pro's and con's for

adopting each course of action

- *Take a breather:* Look at your list of problems and solutions. Ensure that each solution has some pro's and con's attached to it. Leave the list for a day or so
- *Select solutions and make an action plan:* Once you have 'slept on it', select from your list of solutions a number of possible courses of action. It may be necessary at this point to rate the options on a scale of 0-10 in terms of ease of application and the priority you attach to them. Once you have done this, give yourself time to draw up an action plan and ensure that you have, where necessary, a realistic timetable to achieve it
- *Implementation:* Implement your action plan and give it a reasonable period of time to see whether it is effective. At the time of setting the action plan, you should decide how long you are going to try with this course of action before making an evaluation
- *Evaluation:* After a predetermined period reflect on your progress. If progress is not what you expect, repeat the relevant parts of the preceding six steps.

Type-A behaviour and the principles of time management

This pattern of behaviour was first described by two American cardiologists, Meyer Freidman and Ray Rosenman, who made the link between heart disease and behavioural patterns. Essentially, type-A behaviour consists of three characteristics. The first is a great

TABLE 4 **Characteristics of Type-A behaviour**

Prime characteristics	Manifestations
Great determination or obsession to reach goals	Little satisfaction gained from achievement
Sense of urgency	Trying to do too many things at once Eating too quickly Struggling against the clock Impatience
High levels of anger and hostility	Not always shown outwardly but occasional 'explosions'.

determination, which can border on an obsession, to reach goals, but deriving little satisfaction from attainments.

The second is a sense of time urgency, characterised by putting more and more into less and less time. This is exemplified by individuals who try to do more than one thing at a time, eat their food very quickly, or who are engaged in a constant and impatient struggle against other people's routines and the clock!

The third characteristic of such individuals is a high level of anger and hostility which is, for much of the time, often not outwardly directed. However, this anger may occasionally explode, often to the amazement of others.

For a long time it was thought that these characteristics (i.e. the whole type-A behaviour pattern), was the cause of coronary heart disease but research has now shown the picture to be much less clear. Of course, people with type-A behaviour may also be the same people who take little exercise because they do not have enough time, who drink too much alcohol, eat unhealthy food and who may be prone to chain smoking cigarettes. All of these things are factors which have been shown to be responsible for high levels of cardiovascular disease.

Health psychologists have developed programmes which, rather than attempting to abolish type-A behaviour, approach the problem from the stance of modification thus assuming that some people exhibiting this behaviour pattern can indeed be productive and happy. It is simply the extent to which this behaviour is manifested which is the issue.

Time management

One of the key principles which may be used to modify type-A behaviour for the better is that of time management. There is of course no single approach to this issue but it is generally agreed that effective time management should consist of three central elements (Table 5).

1. *Setting of reasonable and at the same time, attainable goals for oneself.* These goals can be divided into the short, the medium and the long term. It is often useful to discuss these goals with another party, who will be able to advise on whether they are indeed reasonable and attainable. For this reason, it is extremely helpful to build in discussions of this sort into the staff appraisal processes used by all major organisations.

Although some professions, such as nursing or teaching, may at first sight be rather difficult to examine in this way, careful consideration of one's role will always produce examples of goals to be attained.

TABLE 5 **Principles of time management**

- Set reasonable but attainable goals in the short, medium and long term
- Establish daily or weekly priorities
- Allow adequate time for individual activities and allow for interruptions
- Be flexible

For example, there may be personal development goals, such as attending specific courses or seminars; a teacher may set himself or herself the goal of designing a new set of lectures with new material or teaching methods; a nurse may enlist the help of a colleague to achieve the goal of being more efficient at carrying out a specific nursing procedure. This approach will necessitate regular practice of the procedure and feedback from the colleague regarding progress.

2. *Set daily and weekly priorities.* In this way one will then need to make the decision about what particular jobs can be left to the following week and, again, one may often need the assistance of a colleague to give the view about whether one's list of tasks is reasonable and realistic.

There is no doubt that management systems need to enable staff to manage their time much more and to also allow for people reaching their true potential. This can help the individual feel that they are in charge of what they do and this will lead to a greater self-esteem. However, this approach also means that there should be easy access to support and supervision from colleagues and managers.

3. *Set a reasonable time for each activity and also allow for unexpected interruptions.* Therefore one's schedule for the day or week must be flexible enough to accommodate the unexpected situation which demands that something else be attended to.

The principles of time management are simple, but the application is often difficult. It is, therefore, helpful to offer staff time management courses and to recognise that time management processes should be built into the reorganisation of work. For that reason, the ward sister or charge nurse should keep these principles uppermost and be aware of the need to assert themselves on behalf of their staff who may, on occasions, be overburdened. The same applies to heads of departments in schools or elsewhere although there is no doubt that in the contemporary scene, as indeed in all areas of working life, people are being increasingly burdened.

However, the time management process can at least allow one to plan and to define what one can and cannot do. A major source of stress is being overwhelmed by the amount of work one needs to do, but not being able to quite define exactly what one's limits are. Sometimes precise knowledge about what is or isn't realistic is enough to retain a sense of control over one's job.

Relaxation training

Relaxation training is but one way of reducing the consequences of physiological arousal. While there are many varieties of relaxation training, most focus on a systematic method of tensing and relaxing the muscles of the body. This has two benefits: first, relaxation training can help the person identify the difference between states of tension and relaxation and, importantly, to recognise when their levels of muscle tension are increasing. Second, there is a considerable amount of evidence to suggest that the systematic tensing and relaxing exercises, eventually lead to a state of overall muscle relaxation and a consequent feeling of well-being.

The following instructions can be followed easily and one simple method may be to read and digest these instructions and then make yourself a cassette, which you can follow. This may be as effective as any of the commercially available tapes and is certainly worth trying before investing hard-earned money!

First of all, find a time in the day when you can spend 30 minutes to give to this task. Find a quiet room, take the phone off the hook and wear loose, comfortable clothing. The exercises can be done in a comfortable chair or lying down and you should experiment with different situations and times of the day to clarify what the optimum conditions are for you.

Before doing the exercises, it is important to remember that when tensing one's muscles, this should be done at a reasonable level; if you tense them too hard you will defeat the object of the exercise. A simple guide is that tensing should lead to no more than a sensation of tension or "pulling"; therefore if you experience pain you are trying too hard! Further, when you release the tension, this release should be immediate. If you are making a tape for yourself, remember that there should be a 10 second gap between each phase.

- Begin with the right hand, clench your fist and do so until your knuckles are white.

  Hold this for 5 seconds and then release immediately.

Pause, wait 10 seconds, repeat exercise.

- Tense your forearm, close your fist and tense the muscles of your forearm. Remember not too hard.

  Hold this for 5 seconds and then release immediately.

  Pause, wait 10 seconds, repeat exercise.

- Tense your biceps, clench your fist and bend your arm to 90^0, concentrate on making your biceps muscle bulge as much as possible.

  Hold this for 5 seconds and then release immediately.

  Pause, wait 10 seconds, repeat exercise.

Repeat the exercises for the left hand, forearm and biceps muscle, remembering to do each exercise twice, hold for 10 seconds and release immediately.

- Tense your eye muscles. Screw up your eyes, hold your eyes shut tight.

  Hold this for 5 seconds and then release immediately.

  Pause, wait 10 seconds, repeat exercise.

- Tense your mouth by clenching your jaws together, concentrate on pushing your lips as firmly together as possible. At the same time you will notice that you will tense your eyes.

  Hold this for 5 seconds and then release immediately.

  Pause, wait 10 seconds, repeat exercise.

- Now concentrate on tensing your neck, push your chin down a little towards your chest but do not touch your chest with your chin.

- Push your shoulders up slightly and tense your neck. Feel the muscles tighten down into your shoulders.

  Hold this for 5 seconds and then release immediately.

  Pause, wait 10 seconds, repeat exercise.

- Tense your shoulders by pushing your arms down, holding your neck rigid and concentrate on tensing across your shoulders.

  Hold this for 5 seconds and then release immediately.

  Pause, wait 10 seconds, repeat exercise.

- Tense the muscles in your back by pushing your elbows into your side, pushing your shoulders down, holding your neck tight, your head down towards your chest and concentrate on tensing the big muscles across your back tense.

  Hold this for 5 seconds and then release immediately.

  Pause, wait 10 seconds, repeat exercise.

- Tense the muscles of your chest by pushing your shoulders back, pushing your elbows down into your waist, tilting your head back slightly and concentrate on holding your chest in a barrel-like, rigid way.

  Hold this for 5 seconds and then release immediately.

  Pause, wait 10 seconds, repeat exercise.

- Tense the muscles of your stomach from the back and pushing towards your navel.

  Hold this for 5 seconds and then release immediately.

Pause, wait 10 seconds, repeat exercise.

- Tense your thighs and buttocks, push your buttocks down, concentrate on tensing your thighs and buttocks together.

  Hold this for 5 seconds and then release immediately.

  Pause, wait 10 seconds, repeat exercise.

- Tense your right calf by pulling your toes up towards you, keeping your legs straight at the knee. Pull your toes back until you can feel a pull all the way up your calf muscles.

  Hold this for 5 seconds and then release immediately.

  Pause, wait 10 seconds, repeat exercise.

- Tense your right foot by curling over your toes, trying to make your toes clench like a fist.

  Hold this for 5 seconds and then release immediately.

  Pause, wait 10 seconds, repeat exercise.

  Repeat sequence for left calf and left foot.

- When you come to the end of these exercises, begin to tense your whole body, starting with your hands, working up through your arms, then head, neck, shoulders, back, chest, stomach, buttocks, thighs, calf and feet.

- Take 10 seconds to gradually tense the whole body.

  Hold for 5 seconds and relax.

- As you relax, breathe out as much as you can with your eyes closed and say 'Calm' to yourself.

Repeat this sequence five times leaving 10 seconds between each cycle.

At this point concentrate on slowing down your breathing, trying to fill all of your chest and as you breathe out, say the word 'calm' to yourself.

Let your breathing settle down into a natural rhythm and then try to fix your mind on a quiet and relaxing scene. Imagine yourself lying on a beach or in a meadow. Imagine a warm atmosphere around you. Try to imagine the smells of such an environment. Keep your mind as fixed as possible and let yourself drift as much as you can.

If you fall asleep, do not worry but perhaps it may be worth setting an alarm clock!

Over-breathing and dealing with hyperventilation

One of the common consequences of encountering stressful situations is over-breathing, or hyperventilation. Normally, if one encounters a dangerous situation, over-breathing is helpful as an increase in respiration will provide the body with the additional oxygen it requires. Most of us will recognise that we will over-breathe when faced with short-term acute stress; this is exemplified by the way people place their hand to their chest when they have encountered some sort of surprise or shock. However, if one is subjected to stress over a long period of time, the over-breathing that occurs can become a problem in its own right.

Put simply, breathing in excess of bodily requirements over a long period leads to an imbalance in body chemistry. An increase in our rate of breathing leads to a reduction in the carbon dioxide levels in the body which, in turn, changes the acid-alkali balance. The consequence of this is that we begin to experience sensations such as pins and needles, feeling light headed, yawning or sighing and in the extreme, developing muscle spasms. Over-breathing also commonly causes fatigue and sleepiness. These symptoms in themselves can be frightening and recurrent attacks of pins and needles may lead the person to think that they are about to have a stroke, or are in the early stages of developing multiple sclerosis. This worry, in turn, produces more stress and thus increases the vicious circle.

However, there is some research evidence to show that some people who suffer panic attacks can be helped by teaching them to breathe more appropriately, thus reducing their hyperventilation and preventing the symptoms which increase their anxiety.

How does one deal with hyperventilation?

Generally speaking, hyperventilation is characterised by an increase in respiration but the pattern of breathing in hyperventilation also changes so that breathing is restricted to the upper part of the chest. Simple breathing exercises, consisting of taking slow but not too deep breaths, can be extremely helpful. Ensure that your breathing is from the diaphragm rather than from the top of the chest. This can be achieved by placing your hand on your abdomen, slightly below the rib cage to ensure that as much of the chest as possible is used.

Generally speaking, sufferers of chronic hyperventilation can reverse this by practising slow diaphragmatic breathing once or twice a day, combining this with a period of physical relaxation. Sometimes people with chronic hyperventilation can be helped by undertaking an exercise, such as running or swimming, as a regular part of their daily programme, but ensuring that this exercise is carried out at a reasonable level. One simple guiding principle is that if you are jogging, for example, you should be able to hold a conversation with a partner. If you are unable to say a few words, you are running too fast! More about exercise follows below.

Hyperventilation in an extreme form may occur during panic attacks and may sometimes produce a range of symptoms which frightens the sufferer and those around him or her. There are some important principles which should be followed to deal with this acute problem.

One should stop whatever one is doing and either sit or lie down in a quiet place. There should be an emphasis on taking slow breaths from the diaphragm as indicated above, and it is helpful to loosen clothing and try to relax one's posture. In this context, try to relax your hands and arms by shaking them. This will also help to stop you hunching up your shoulders which, in itself, increases hyperventilation.

One very rapid and effective way of dealing with the problem is to re-breathe expired air. Expired air contains more carbon dioxide than the air around us and this replenishing of the carbon dioxide in the body's carbon dioxide reverses the chemical changes which follow from hyperventilation. The very old trick of breathing in and out of a paper bag is the most effective, but this is not always possible in all situations. A simple alternative is to cup your hands over your nose and mouth and re-breathe the expired air in this way. Doing this for two to three minutes is generally be enough to restore the correct chemical balance in the body.

If you are in the company of someone who hyperventilates, one of the key principles in managing this problem is to remain calm yourself. It is important to remember that hyperventilation rarely, if ever, leads to any permanent medical consequence, although in very extreme and unusual circumstances the person affected may go into violent muscular spasm. Even this spasm is generally harmless as the condition (known as tetany) is self-limiting and is the body's way of stopping the over-breathing until the chemical balance begins to be restored. Stay with the person, ensure they remain still, try to help them relax their muscles and emphasise the need to breath slowly and from the diaphragm. Using the paper bag trick or cupped hands to re-breathe expired air should also be emphasised.

Exercise

There is of course a wide range of evidence to show that exercise, taken regularly and sensibly, reduces the risk of coronary heart disease, hypertension and possibly some sorts of cancer. However, it is also clear that people who exercise regularly report lesser levels of anxiety, tension and depression. Is this because exercise reduces stress or is it simply that people who lead less stressful lifestyles have more time to exercise? The answer to this seems clear. A considerable amount of research suggests that, regardless of background or lifestyle, regular moderate exercise not only increases cardiovascular fitness but also reduces levels of anxiety and depression.

The important thing to emphasise here is that it is *moderate* exercise that produces these results; lower level exercise, such as badminton, golf or even very long walks, does not have the same significant effect. A round of golf or an hours' walk may indeed produce a sense of well-being because of the distracting nature of the activity but there is little doubt that the deeper and longer lasting effects which accrue to more strenuous exercise do not happen at this level.

Of course, those under stress often argue that they have no time for exercise and, indeed, that if they took the time, their level of stress would increase! This is a rather false argument as it is likely that regular exercise will increase well-being, reduce anxiety and, therefore, increase concentration and efficiency. In the long term, therefore, taking time out to exercise regularly may be actually cost efficient. It is also a matter of priority because there is clearly no contest between achieving the heights of business success and dying at the age of 45, as compared with, perhaps, being marginally less committed, but nevertheless successful and leading an active life well into one's middle or late years.

How much exercise should one take to reduce stress?

The key principle with all exercise programmes is that of graduation. If you have not exercised at all for a long time, it is obviously wise to start slowly and, although many advise that advice should be sought from a doctor before commencing an exercise programme, unless one is vastly obese or has a serious medical problem, there seems little reason why a medical consultation is necessary, providing that the programme begins gradually.

For example, alternately jogging and walking for a period of ten minutes twice a week can really be undertaken by anybody. You should jog, until you becomes breathless, walk until you regain your breath and then start off again. This pattern stands more chance of success if done in company and for those with the opportunity a simple programme can often be planned and developed at a local sports centre for little or no cost.

The best exercise is found in sports such as running, swimming, rowing, cycling, where one generally attains a certain level of activity and keeps at that plateau for a reasonable period of time. The eventual aim should be to exercise at least three times a week for a minimum of 20 minutes at this level. The rule of thumb about the level to be aimed for is that you should undertake the sort of activity which gets you to the point of being breathless, but just able to say a few words.

For the more technically minded, there are various formulae for calculating optimum exercise rates from your heart rate. Heart rate monitors are now widely used by exercisers of all levels although the simple taking of one's pulse can be just as effective. One reasonable calculation is that one should aim for 70-80% of one's maximum heart rate. The maximum heart rate is generally thought to be 220 minus one's age and thus a 40 year old should aim for exercise which gets the heart rate to between 130-140 per minute and keeps it at this level for a reasonable period.

One difficulty with exercise is that one can get bored so that longer term strategies should be considered. Exercising in company, joining a club and varying one's sports are all different ways of maintaining the habit. Generally speaking, the problems of maintaining a good exercise pattern are likely to occur in the first few weeks or months rather than once the habit has become established.

There are, of course, some notes of caution - the principal one being that people who have very high levels of stress and who find that exercise produces relief can, on occasion find themselves becoming addicted to exercise. One does come across cases of people who end up exercising to the point that their physical health is impaired and this, of course, a problem in its own right.

However, exercise is one of the most important of the stress-management strategies and can provide a great improvement in the quality of one's life.

Identifying negative thoughts - the role of diary keeping

Sometimes keeping a diary can be a useful way of isolating some of the causes of stress and can help define an overall pattern which may not previously have been evident. A diary is also helpful in examining more objectively one's specific response to circumstances. For example, it may be that encounters with other people lead to a pattern of negative thinking (e.g. 'I'm sure that this person thinks I'm hopeless' or 'No-one cares what I think').

Keeping a diary over a period of time may show that there are consistent negative reactions to a range of events so that a diary kept over, say, 3-4 weeks may reveal an habitual negative response to circumstances. You can then take action to overcome this.

A suggested diary format is shown in Table 6. This may help to show a clear pattern and, once a reasonable amount of information is collected, you can then look at the thoughts in a more rational way. For example, you are walking along the corridor at work and a colleague does not return your greeting, a classic negative response may be that the colleague thinks that you are not worth talking to, or you may feel that you have done something to upset him. Further scrutiny of your diary may reveal that in other encounters you interpret various words and actions in a negative way.

Taking the example of not returning your greeting, some alternative explanations may be that your colleague was so engrossed in his own

TABLE 6 **Keeping a 'stress diary'**

Specific situation	Thoughts and feelings	Consequences	Anxiety and mood ratings

problems that he did not see you, that he was preoccupied by a work issue, or even that he was uncertain of what to say and ended up saying nothing.

In a similar vein, you may find that when I look at your diary, I see that you always catastrophise about forthcoming social events, worrying that you may make a fool of yourself, may not be able to cope with the conversation and so on. Examination of the diary may reveal that in the event you always perform well. This very simple sort of objective analysis can often help to correct negative perceptions. It may be that adding another column to the diary to add your rational response to the initial thought may be helpful in training you to think in a more realistic and positive fashion. This form of diary keeping is one of the central strands of a new approach to treating depression and anxiety, called cognitive therapy.

Sleep

For many people sleep disturbance is one of the first manifestations of problems in life. This can take many forms. Anxiety usually leads to difficulties getting off to sleep and frequent awakening during the night. Classically, in depression, people fall asleep fairly quickly but wake in the early hours of the morning, unable to get back to sleep and racked by guilt and/or negative and catastrophic thoughts. Sometimes sleep disturbance produces further problems. For example, if you have had two or three nights of broken sleep, it is easy to see how you can develop a self-fulfilling prophecy in worrying about the next night's sleep - this worry then keeps you awake!

Furthermore, sleeping problems are often compounded by the use of drugs and alcohol. Alcohol, in particular, will promote sleep but, when the effects wear off, one often wakes feeling pretty rotten and miserable in the early hours of the morning, having experienced a very artificial and, in effect, drug-induced state of stupor. Sleeping tablets are generally not helpful beyond the first few nights of taking them as the body quickly adapts to their chemical effects. Unfortunately many people become addicted to sleeping tablets and find themselves unable to manage without their assistance.

What can one do about sleeping problems?

First of all there are some fairly simple questions to pose. For example: Is my mattress in need of changing? How long is it since I bought a new pillow? Is the heating and ventilation in the bedroom adequate? Does my partner snore and keep me awake (in this case, sending your partner to another room or to the doctor for a cure for snoring may be the answer!).

One should also examine one's eating habits (see page 40) and sometimes eating too late may cause a problem, as may the ingestion of strong tea or coffee late in the evening. By contrast one may find that a hot milky drink taken late at night is useful.

The other important factor to consider is exercise. Obviously plenty of physical exercise can assist sleep considerably but, for some people, exercise in the evening will interfere with sleep and thus they need to reconsider the timing of this routine.

There has been a considerable amount of research activity in the treatment of sleep problems over the last 30 years, much of which is taking place in the USA. We still do not know why we sleep, but it seems essential that we take between seven and nine hours per night. As a point of interest there is some evidence that many people who sleep much less than this have a reduced life expectancy. However it is worth emphasising here that although a reduction in sleep is a common manifestation of stress, some people under stress tend to sleep more. Sleeping too much can certainly lead to depression and there is research evidence to show that reducing a pattern of sleeping too much can have very significant (and beneficial) effects on mood.

Several methods have been applied to the management of sleeping problems which do not involve the use of drugs. First, relaxation training can be of considerable benefit and undertaking the exercises shown on page 22 may assist a significant number of people with sleeping difficulties. Techniques called autogenic training and biofeedback training have also been applied. There are variations on relaxation methods, such as: biofeedback which involves the use of electronic equipment which measures various states of body tension and autogenic training which represents an attempt to reprogram the body's automatic response by emphasis on muscle relaxation.

However, one of the simplest methods of dealing with sleep problems is an approach called 'Sleep Hygiene' or 'Stimulus Control' which simply involves applying a number of simple rules to one's sleep routine and also makes the assumption that poor sleeping patterns are caused or made worse by not conforming to these rules. The following steps should be applied and although some of them may sound harsh, it is well worth trying to stick to all of the principles:

- *Get up at a set time every day.* This should be the same seven days a week. This strategy is aimed at training the body to conform to a natural cycle.
- *Only go to bed when feeling sleepy and about to 'drop off'.* Going to bed when you are not sleepy and forcing oneself to try to go to sleep will make the problem worse. Sometimes those with sleeping problems feel that if they go to bed earlier, even if they are not sleepy, they will give themselves the opportunity to 'catch up'. However, this rarely works, and more usually leads to a pattern of 'tossing and turning'. Put simply , if you maintain the first rule and get up at the same time each day, and go to bed only when you are sleepy, the body will quickly find its natural cycle.
- *Take no naps during the day.* Sometimes people with

sleeping problems succumb to the temptation to sleep during the day to 'catch up' on lost sleep. Naps are, of course, very pleasant for people without sleeping problems, but if one has such a difficulty, a nap will disrupt the natural cycle and inhibit the onset of natural sleep at night.

- *Do nothing else in the bedroom other than sleep.* Sometimes people with sleep problems equip their bedrooms with a range of reading materials, television, radio, compact disc player, etc.. The use of these appliances will tend to reinforce a pattern of staying awake and, of course, runs completely contrary to the idea of feeling sleepy and going immediately to bed to sleep.

Over the years when using this approach with patients, I have emphasised that the instruction to do nothing else in the bedroom other than sleep is supported by the exception that sexual activity is allowed and this is a very good way of inducing a sleepy state!

- *Do not lie in bed and toss and turn even if you cannot sleep.* If you wake up in the middle of the night, the worst thing that you can do is to toss and turn. Therefore, if you wake up and are not able to go back to sleep fairly quickly, you should remove yourself from the bedroom, go to another area and undertake a fairly neutral activity. Do something like a crossword, tapestry or play patience. If you become sleepy again, you should then return to bed. Otherwise, you should stay up, even if that means not returning to bed again that night.

In the early days this programme may cause some difficulty, but if you stick to the five rules, generally speaking, within a very short

TABLE 7 **The 'five rules' for dealing with sleeping problems**

- Get up at the same time every day
- Only go to bed when feeling ready to sleep
- Take no naps during the day
- Do nothing other than sleep in the bedroom
- When unable to sleep at night get up and do something else; return to bed only when ready to sleep.

space of time, the body takes over and the natural sleep cycle becomes embedded.

Stimulus control can be assisted by a relaxation training programme and it may also be helpful to ban all caffeinated drinks and alcohol for a trial period to reduce over-stimulation. Stimulus control rules are, if you think about it, very natural ways of overcoming a problem which troubles most of us at some time. Such an approach is, in the longer term, much more effective and infinitely more preferable than 'popping a pill'.

Diet

People under stress usually eat badly and, although it is obvious, it is worth pointing out that hurried eating patterns and an unbalanced diet can make their problem worse. Thus, for someone who is already under stress, and potentially at risk from high blood pressure, their problems can be compounded by the intake of large quantities of fat which may 'clog up' the arteries. Therefore, dealing with your diet is an essential part of managing your stress.

Setting aside a sensible time to eat one's lunch may seem like an intrusion into a busy daily routine, but taking ¾hr. out of a busy day to enjoy a pleasant meal may, in fact, enhance one's performance in the long run. An obvious benefit of healthy eating is a consequent reduction in weight and increase in self-esteem. Eating is, of course, one of our most fundamental activities and must therefore never be overlooked. You are what (and how) you eat.

Here are some simple rules which will make your eating healthier and probably also more enjoyable:

- Eat plenty of carbohydrate (pasta, bread, rice and potatoes).
- Ensure your diet contains sufficient fibre. This will also help you to feel satisfied for longer. Therefore eat unrefined carbohydrate such as wholemeal or granary bread, eat potatoes and their skins, eat beans and use dried and fresh fruit as a snack food.
- Avoid refined foods (e.g. sugar, white bread, fast foods).
- Eat five portions of fresh fruit and fresh vegetables every day.
- Reduce or cut out red meat and offal (e.g. kidneys, hearts).
- Reduce your fat intake (grill foods rather than frying them, use skimmed rather than full fat milk, eat cheese once or twice a week only)
- Try to eat three or four meals a day; be sure that you start with a good breakfast - fruit and cereal is good! Avoid snacks but if you must, eat fruit or vegetables (dried, fresh or frozen)

- Give yourself a minimum of 30 minutes to eat your meal.
- Reduce your speed of eating, put your knife and fork down between mouthfuls, concentrating instead on chewing and enjoying the taste.
- Eat with a companion if you can.
- Don't eat your last meal too late, and take a gentle walk after this meal if you can.

Alcohol

The use of alcohol is widespread and, unfortunately, it is often used unwisely by people under stress. It seems to provide an instant solution. Alcohol makes one feel physically relaxed, gets one off to sleep and can provide a temporary respite. However, in excess, alcohol can cause a variety of problems, the detailed discussion of which is out of place here. Suffice it to say that alcohol represents a major public health problem with an estimated 1,000,000 people whose lives are adversely affected by alcohol consumption. Alcohol is the biggest cause of homicide being implicated as a factor in over 50% of all murders. It leads to thousands of road fatalities and causes immeasurable problems in the workplace. At an individual level it can cause a wide range of physical problems and it is estimated that up to one third of admissions to in-patient medical facilities are linked to excessive alcohol use.

Signs of an alcohol problem; what can be done about it?

Everybody recognises the stereotypical alcoholic who has lost home and family and behaves in an antisocial and disorganised fashion.

However, the vast majority of people with alcohol problems do not conform in any way to this stereotype. That is not to say, however, that their lives are not sometimes catastrophically affected. There are many signs that alcohol is causing a problem. There are several questions that one should ask oneself:

- Do I drink every day?
- Has my tolerance for alcohol changed (i.e. am I drinking more than before to get the same effect?) or has my capacity increased or decreased?
- Do I feel guilty because of my drinking?
- Do I have memory gaps?
- Do friends comment on the amount I drink?
- Do I sometimes feel shaky after a heavy drinking session?
- Do I exceed the safe drinking limit? This is 21 units for a man per week and 14 units for a woman. A unit represents half a pint of beer, a pub measure of spirit or a normal sized glass of wine. There has been some controversy about what constitutes a safe level, but there is little doubt that individuals who consume greater than the above figures have a statistically greater chance of developing health problems or of suffering social or legal consequences.

One of the great difficulties with answering these questions is that those who have, or are in the midst of, developing an alcohol problem, and this includes people in the very early stages, often rationalise their circumstances. They may say for example, 'I wouldn't drink so much if my boss was nicer to me' or 'Anyone would drink if they had my pressures' or they deny these problems completely. Take a long hard look at the questions and if the answer to any one of these is 'yes', you should consider seriously that you may have a problem.

At lower levels, alcohol problems can be dealt with by modifying one's drinking pattern but, if there are signs of physical dependence or any significant gaps in memory, the best course of action is to seek professional treatment or to attend Alcoholics Anonymous with a view to permanently abstaining from alcohol.

However, for the majority of people who are drinking too much and who do not have the serious signs noted above, there are a number of strategies which are worth trying. Application of these strategies will often restore normal drinking. Indeed, we must remember that alcohol taken at a reasonable level does provide a number of very positive social and psychological advantages. For example, small quantities of alcohol will reduce inhibition and facilitate interaction and small amounts of alcohol will assist the process of relaxation. Alcohol is nature's oldest relaxant and, if used sparingly, is probably much more effective than any tranquillisers!

The important principles are as follows:

- Give yourself an allowance, not exceeding 21 units per week if you are a man and 14 units per week if you are a woman (don't consume all of this in one session!)
- Always aim to have at least 2/3 drink free days per week
- Space your drinks. Try to ensure that you never consume more than one unit per half hour. If you are at a wedding or party which goes on for several hours, space your drinks using non-alcoholic drinks in between, or dilute your wine

with mineral water, or your beer with lemonade

- Never drink alone
- Unless it is a social event which is out of the ordinary, do not drink during the day. Do not drink during working hours.

These principles should be seriously applied over a period of at least three months. Drinking should be monitored honestly using a diary, recording the amounts in units. If, at the end of this time, you still answer yes to the above questions, you should certainly seek advice from either your doctor, one of the local alcohol advisory centres or Alcoholics Anonymous (the local addresses of which can be found in your GP surgery, library or telephone book); the National line is listed at the end of this book.

Smoking

Smoking is one of the most maladaptive ways of dealing with stress and is the cause of a whole array of illnesses. People under stress often say that smoking is something they will give up when they feel better but, because of the lethal nature of this habit and, because no time is a good time for giving up, smoking cessation should be seen as a priority.

There are now an increasing number of 'quit smoking' programmes and help lines (see addresses at the end of this book), but the overwhelming evidence seems to be that smoking cessation programmes are enhanced by the use of nicotine chewing gum or patches. Furthermore your family doctor should now have easy access to smoking cessation programmes and many of the larger practices or health centres will run their own, usually with the assistance of a practice nurse. Detailed advice is out of place in a book such as this; however the following are worth trying:

- Set a day for giving up.
- Prior to that day, change the pattern of your smoking. For example, do without the cigarette after your meals, leave a longer stub, ban yourself from smoking in certain places.
- Keep a record of every cigarette smoked, write down a tick on a notepad when you take one from the packet - ask yourself if it is really necessary.
- Don't empty the ashtrays at home or in the car - remind yourself of the aftermath.
- Write down monthly the money you spend on cigarettes.
- When attempting to stop use nicotine chewing gum or patches, but do follow the advice on the leaflets carefully.
- Stop with a friend or relative.
- Learn a relaxation procedure.
- Put the money you save in a place where it is visible (e.g. a glass jar).
- Stock your fridge with fruit, diet drinks and vegetables. Use these liberally when you crave a cigarette.
- If you start again, don't give up trying to give up!

Assertion training

Stress may be induced by the inability to handle interpersonal problems so that you should examine the way you get on with other people to see whether some of the sources of stress may simply derive from your inability to say 'No'. For example, stress at work may often be accounted for by an individual taking on more and more and in effect having less and less time to complete tasks. This, in turn, produces poor performance and then poor self-esteem because you have not done your job to the usual standards.

Similarly, communicating your feelings to your manager at work is important. You may, for example, have a manager who has little time because of the nature and size of their own job and duties but it is nevertheless important to communicate feelings of dissatisfaction or unhappiness to them.

The answers to situations such as this are sometimes not straightforward and learning to say no may be a very difficult thing for some people to do. If, however, this and other areas of communication are difficult, it is well worth while trying to find an assertion training course, perhaps run by a local authority or an employer. In these courses people meet for a defined period of, say, 10 sessions over as many weeks and spend the sessions in role play, (i.e. acting out real life situations) and in looking at various ways of dealing with problems. Such training provides practice in the relevant techniques and may be assisted by video feedback. Although this may cause some initial embarrassment, seeing yourself as others see you is extremely valuable. Video is increasingly used as a tool in this area.

More simply there are now a large number of excellent books on assertion. Many of these are, like this book, based on the principle of self-help. Any large book store will provide a wide choice.

Hobbies

People under stress , and particularly those whose jobs are the main source of the problem, will very often neglect their hobbies and interests. They do this because they feel that hobbies and interests erode the time they need to give to work. This is a false economy as diverse interests keep one's mind fresh and flexible. Furthermore, absorption in something from which you derive happiness and/or satisfaction will lead to an increase in self-esteem which will carry over into the job area. When things go wrong at work hobbies also provide a useful escape and, if one has a number of interests and hobbies, work becomes but one area rather than the only area of life. Although pointing to hobbies and interests is obvious, it is one of those things that does need some emphasis. There are two simple questions you can ask yourself: What interests and hobbies was I involved in 10 years ago? Why did I stop doing them?

PROFESSIONAL HELP

Some forms of stress, of course, require professional help but most people can achieve significant reduction in the effect of stress by applying some of the principles described in this book. However, if the stress causes consistent physical symptoms, causes continuing problems with work and/or social and personal relationships despite the application of self help methods, it may be worth asking for some professional assistance.

Many organisations now run stress management courses and these may be extremely helpful. However, help can also be accessed via your general practitioner, who may be able to refer you to a suitable stress management programme. Indeed, some general practices provide courses within their own surgeries. These programmes may be run by clinical psychologists, suitably trained nurses, occupational therapists and others. Accepting professional help is not a sign of failure. Sometimes even the most able person needs a health professional to help them to help themselves.

The role of medication

Although medication is certainly not a first-line approach to stress problems, it may be necessary in certain cases. For example, where stress leads to an increase in blood pressure (also called hypertension) your general practitioner may wish to prescribe a medication from the group of drugs called the beta blockers. This treatment may be necessary for a few weeks, months or indefinitely. These drugs sometimes lead to a very helpful reduction in anxiety, although one should also include other approaches to both look at the source of stress and to deal with its effects. Indeed, there is evidence that for the less serious forms of hypertension, relaxation training can be as effective as medication. However, in this case, this needs to be done with the consent (and under the supervision of) your GP.

People who have experienced significant and long standing stress may develop depression and, in some cases, a suitable anti-depressant drug may be necessary. If you have experienced weight loss, show very marked changes in your pattern of sleep, appetite or sexual interest, an anti-depressant medication is certainly worth considering. There are now new generations of anti-depressant drugs (e.g. Prozac) which have many fewer side effects than the older compounds and which do not seem to have any significant risk of addiction.

However, if one embarks on anti-depressant medication, one should know that most doctors will wish you to take it for several months and this includes a period after you have felt a return to normal. This seems to be necessary because anti-depressants can be looked upon as a way of adjusting the body's chemistry to alter the deleterious effects of stress. In turn, this adjustment needs to be undertaken over a long-term period and given over a sufficient period of time to allow the body to reach its own equilibrium.

OTHER APPROACHES

There are other approaches to the management of stress. For example, meditation of which there are a number of different forms, may be a useful alternative to relaxation training and some studies have shown that meditation can significantly reduce blood pressure levels. In a similar vein, some of the martial arts have been used to achieve physical relaxation and seem to provide an excellent mixture of mental discipline and physical exercise.

Hypnosis is a treatment that is still widely popular and many people with anxiety disorders ask for hypnosis when they attend mental health professionals for treatment. There is no doubt that the hypnotic state really does exist and the recordings of the brainwaves of individuals under hypnosis show characteristic differences from the normal waking state. However, hypnotic states are probably not much different to those states achieved by muscle relaxation training and, although there are many extravagant claims for efficacy, research has so far been unable to demonstrate any long lasting effects on anxiety states or stress conditions over and above that which can be achieved by the use of placebos.

As stress is a very difficult entity to define, the treatment for stress-related conditions is difficult to evaluate. However, procedures such as relaxation training, problem-oriented counselling and hyper-ventilation have all been researched within the context of properly conducted clinical trials and, although these techniques are far from panaceas for all forms of stress, they have been shown to be effective for specific conditions.

With regard to some of the 'complementary medicine' approaches there is unfortunately little in the way of controlled evaluation. The one exception to this is acupuncture, which is fast becoming integral to mainstream medicine and, although the underlying physiological mechanisms of acupuncture are poorly understood, it is now becoming much more accepted as a validated treatment. However, at the moment, the effects of acupuncture on anxiety conditions remain unclear and, in my view, this approach should be used cautiously.

Other complementary approaches, such as aromatherapy, reflexology and herbal medicine have enthusiastic support from some quarters. There is still virtually no definitive research evidence to attest to their effectiveness. There is, however, a great deal of anecdotal evidence that aromatherapy and reflexology in particular lead to states of relaxation at the time when they are applied, although how such results can be generalised to every day life is not clear.

My simple advice regarding these approaches is that they are worth a try if you have the time and money, but you should try where possible to only go to practitioners who have properly accredited training. You should also ask at the outset how long it will be before you can expect results. If the answer is that this is impossible to answer, or the time given is in terms of months rather than weeks, my advice would be to adopt a very cautious attitude.

CONCLUSION

There is no doubt that stress is a universal phenomenon and although it is often seen as the product of modern life, it is to be found in every culture and probably has been present throughout history. This book has attempted to describe some of the approaches which have been shown to be effective in the management of stress and as far as possible I have paid the greater part of my attention to those approaches which have been shown to be effective in properly conducted research. As stated before, no one strategy is a panacea and you may need to use a number of the approaches outlined to deal with your problem. Even then you should not expect miraculous change.

Cure is a word one reserves for the successful treatment of a disease. Stress is often seen as a disease, but is probably better conceptualised as an exaggeration of normality. Therefore approaches must be designed to reduce stress rather than to abolish it. Remember that stress and the various reactions included are adaptive and part of our survival mechanisms. Fight or flight, even in today's society, is a part of day to day life and therefore we must learn to live with it. In the same way one should view stress - if you know what it is and how to control it, your life can be happy and productive. However, if it is currently out of control, read and digest the principles in this book and remember that the vast majority of people can master most of the strategies described here within a few weeks.

FURTHER READING

David Fontana, 1993, Managing Stress, published by BPS Books, London.

David Fontana, 1993, Managing Time, published by BPS Books, London.

George W. Brown and Tirril Harris, 1995, Life Events and Illness: A Handbook for the Caring Professions, published by Unwin Hyman: International Thomson, London.

Isaac Marks, 1978, Living with Fear, published by McGraw Hill Book Company, London.

Ken Powell, 1993, What happens when Stress gets out of Control - and how to regain your Sanity, published by Thorsons, London.

Trevor Powell and Simon Enwright, 1990, Anxiety and Stress Management, published by Tavistock Publications, London.

Margaret Sills and Ann Aris, 1994, Positive Stress at Work, published by the Health Education Authority, London.

Murray Watts and Cary L. Cooper, 1992, Relax - Dealing with Stress, published by BBC Books, London.

Action on Smoking and Health (ASH)

109, Gloucester Place, London W1H 4EJ.

Telephone: 0171 - 935 - 3519

Alcoholics Anonymous

P. O. Box 1, Stonebow House, Stonebow, York YO1 2NJ.

Telephone: 01904 - 644026/7/8/9

Biofeedback

Maxwell Cade Foundation, 9, Chatsworth Road, London NW2 4BJ.

Telephone: 0181 - 451 - 0083

British Association for Autogenic Training and Therapy

18, Holtsmere Close, Garston, Watford, Herts WC2 6NG.

British Association for Counselling

1, Regent Place, Rugby, Warwicks CV21 2PJ.

Telephone: 01788 - 758328

Centre for Stress Management

156, Westcombe Hill, Blackheath, London SE3 7HP.

Council for Acupuncture

179, Gloucester Place, London NW1 6DX.

Telephone: 0171 -724 - 5756

Triumph over Phobia

P O Box 1831, Bath BA1 3YX.

Telephone: 01225 - 330353

Phobia Action

Hornbeam House, Claybury Grounds, Manor Road, Woodford Green, Essex IG8 8PR.

Telephone: 0181 559 2551

TELEPHONE HELPLINES

Alcoholics Anonymous Helpline
Telephone: 0171 - 352 - 3001

SANELINE (information and support for carers, sufferers or friends)
Telephone: 0171 -724 - 8000

SMOKERS QUITLINE
Telephone: 0171 - 487 - 3000